M. Searl.

py

P9-CQN-475

NOTHING DAUNTED

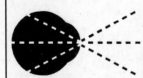

This Large Print Book carries the
Seal of Approval of N.A.V.H.

NOTHING DAUNTED

THE UNEXPECTED EDUCATION OF TWO SOCIETY GIRLS IN THE WEST

DOROTHY WICKENDEN

THORNDIKE PRESS
A part of Gale, Cengage Learning

GALE
CENGAGE Learning·

Detroit • New York • San Francisco • New Haven, Conn • Waterville, Maine • London

GALE
CENGAGE Learning

LIBRARY OF CONGRESS CATALOGING-IN-PUBLICATION DATA

Wickenden, Dorothy.
    Nothing daunted : the unexpected education of two society girls in the
West / by Dorothy Wickenden. — Large print ed.
    p. cm. (Thorndike press large print biography)
    Includes bibliographical references.
    ISBN-13: 978-1-4104-5635-9 (hardcover : large print)
    ISBN-10: 1-4104-5635-8 (hardcover : large print) 1. Woodruff, Dorothy. 2.
Underwood, Rosamond. 3. Teachers—Colorado—Biography. 4.
Education—Colorado—History—20th century. 5. Large type books. I. Title.
LA2315.C59W53 2013
371.100922--dc23
    [B]   2012044220

Published in 2013 by arrangement with Scribner, a division of Simon &
Schuster, Inc.

Printed in the United States of America
1 2 3 4 5 6 7 17 16 15 14 13

for Hermione and Caroline

Rosamond and Dorothy, "Stranded for a day on the Moffat Road"

CONTENTS

PROLOGUE

Miss Underwood (left), Miss Woodruff, and Elkhead students, 1916

One weekend afternoon in the fall of 2008, at the back of a drawer in my old wooden desk at home, I came across a folder I had forgotten. "Dorothy Woodruff Letters, Elkhead 1916–17." My mother had given me

9

the file when my children were young, and I had put it away, intending to look through it, but life had intervened. I glanced at the first letter. Dated Friday, July 28, 1916, it was written on the stationery of the Hayden Inn. At the top of the sheet was a photograph of a homely three-story concrete-block house with a few spindly saplings out front. The inn advertised itself as "The Only First-Class Hotel in Hayden." Dorothy wrote: "My dearest family: Can you believe that I am actually far out here in Colorado?"

She and her close friend, Rosamond Underwood, had grown up together in Auburn, New York. They had just arrived after a five-day journey and were preparing to head into a remote mountain range in the Rockies, to teach school in a settlement called Elkhead. Dorothy's letter described their stop overnight in Denver, their train ride across the Continental Divide, and their introductions to the locals of Hayden, whom she described as "all agog" over them "and *so* funny." One man could barely be restrained "from showing us a bottle of gall stones just removed from his wife!" She closed by saying, "They are all so friendly and kind — and we are *thrilled* by every-thing. We start now — four hours drive. Goodbye in haste. . . ."

Dorothy Woodruff was my grandmother. As I began reading the letters, I recognized her voice immediately, even though they were written by a young woman — twenty-nine years old, unmarried, belatedly setting out on her own. An avid correspondent, she captured the personalities of the people she met; the harsh landscape; her trials with a classroom of unruly young boys; and her devotion to Rosamond, known to my brothers and me as "Aunt Ros." I also was struck by their unusually warm friendship with two men: the young lawyer and rancher who hired them, Farrington Carpenter; and Bob Perry, who was the supervisor of his father's coal mine. They were eighteen hundred miles away from their families, and from decorous notions about relations between the sexes.

The letters revealed the contradictions of Dorothy's upbringing. She was a daughter of the Victorian aristocracy. Her forebears, like Rosamond's, were entrepreneurs and lawyers and bankers who had become wealthy during the Industrial Revolution. In 1906, the young women were sent to Smith, one of the earliest women's colleges, and afterward, they were indulged for a year with a grand tour of Europe, during which they saw their first "aeroplane," learned how

11

to blow the foam off a mug of beer, expressed disdain for the paintings of Matisse, and watched Nijinsky dance. Then, like other girls of their background, they were expected to return home to marry, and marry well.

Yet they had grown up surrounded by the descendants of some of the most prominent reformers in American history, including the suffragists who organized the first women's rights convention in Seneca Falls, fifteen miles west of Auburn; and the man who overturned barbaric penal practices at the Auburn state prison, Sing Sing, and penitentiaries across the country. Auburn was a stop on the Underground Railroad, and some of the families they knew had hidden runaway slaves in their basements. Dorothy's grandfather lived next door to William Seward, President Lincoln's secretary of state. One day when she was visiting my family in Weston, Connecticut, she recorded an oral history, speaking with unerring precision about her childhood and about her time in Colorado. Retrieving the transcript of the tape, I was reminded of the breathtaking brevity of America's past.

I remember Dorothy as white-haired, impeccably attired, and sometimes stern. The second youngest of seven children, she grew up in a big hipped-roof clapboard house staffed by servants. Her bedroom and that of her younger sister, Milly, were in the nursery, reached by the back stairs. Raised largely by their nursemaid, they rarely stepped into the kitchen. When Dorothy's four children were growing up, she didn't know how to cook anything except creamed potatoes and hot cocoa. Every night she brushed her hair a hundred strokes with a French boar-bristle brush. She joked to us about her height — four feet eleven and shrinking every year. To reach her high mahogany four-poster bed, inherited from her parents, she had to use a footstool upholstered in needlepoint.

She gave me tips in etiquette: how to file my nails, how to set a formal table, how to avoid acting "common." When I was a slouching teenager, she showed me how she had been taught to walk across the room with a book balanced on her head. On my eighteenth birthday, she wrote to me: "To be happy it is necessary to be constantly giving to others. I do not mean to give in work alone — but all of your self. That means interest in other people — not only by affection — but by kindness." She didn't like the fashions of the 1970s — curtains of hair, tie-dyed T-shirts, and tight bell-bottoms — and once told me haughtily, "I never wore a pair of trousers in my life."

For all that, she was spirited and funny — not at all the deferential young woman she had been brought up to be. After she and Ros returned from Europe, they attended friends' weddings, along with traditional luncheons and balls, but six years later, they were still uninterested in the suitors who were interested in them. Chafing at the rigid social routines and not getting anywhere with the ineffectual suffrage work they had taken on, they didn't hesitate when they heard about two teaching jobs in Colorado. The nine months my grandmother spent there seemed to have shaped her as much as her entire youth in Auburn. She was full of expansive admiration for the hardworking people of Elkhead, and when she faced great personal difficulties of her own, she called to mind the uncomplaining endurance she had witnessed in the settlers and their children.

She and Ros, like other easterners going west, were time travelers, moving back to the frontier. Although they ventured out after the first settlers, and went by train rather than covered wagon, their destination felt more like 1870 than 1916. They took with them progressive ideas about education, technology, and women — and post-cards from their travels abroad. The home-steaders — motley transplants from across the country, Europe, and Russia — lived almost twenty miles north of Hayden. Effectively cut off from modern life by poverty and the Rocky Mountains, the pioneers found the two women as exotic as Dorothy and Ros found them.

Although World War I was looming, such a cataclysm was unimaginable to Americans who knew nothing of combat. Dorothy sometimes talked disparagingly about her grandfather's brother, who had avoided service in the Civil War by paying a substitute to take his place — a common practice among wealthy families in the North. Just weeks before Dorothy and Ros left for Colorado, President Wilson averted war with Mexico. The prevailing spirit among the elites of Auburn, the industrialists of Denver, and the homesteaders of Elkhead was an exhilarating optimism about the future.

These people were swept up in some of the strongest currents of the country's history: the expulsion of native tribes; the mining of gold, silver, and coal; the building of a network of railroads that linked disparate parts of the country and led to the settlement of the West; the development of rural schools; the entry of immigrants, African-Americans, and women into the workforce and the voting booth; even the origins of modern dance. Their lives were integral to the making of America, yet the communities they built, even their idioms, had all but vanished.

As I got to know the children and grandchildren of the people my grandmother told us about, I began to see her story as more than a curious family history. It was an alternative Western. There were strutting cowboys and eruptions of violence, but the records the residents left behind turned out to be full of their own indelible characters and plot twists. Dozens of descendants in Denver, Steamboat Springs, Hayden, Elkhead, and Oak Creek had kept their family memorabilia from that year. Rebecca Wattles, a rancher in Hayden and the granddaughter of the secretary of the Elkhead school board, showed me the 1920 yearbook of the first five graduates of the school, all of whom had been Ros's students. They wrote: "It isn't the easiest thing in the world to buck trail for two or three miles when the trail is drifted and your horse lunges and plunges; nor yet to ski, when the snow is loose and sticky. But, if as we are told, it is these things that develop grit, stick-to-it-ive-ness, and independence — well, the children who have gone to school in Elk Head, ought surely to have a superfluous amount of those qualities."

One Sunday in early October 2009, my husband and I pulled up to an old white Georgian house on a cul-de-sac in Norwalk, Connecticut. We were greeted at the front door by Peter Cosel, one of Ros's grandsons. He appeared to be mildly amused by my mission: a search for the letters that Rosamond had written from Elkhead. For a year I had been pestering him about going through the boxes he had in storage there. Peter called his brother Rob, also a lawyer, who arrived just as we finished a cursory examination of the attic treasures, including a trunk filled with papers dating back to the 1850s from a branch of the Underwood family that had settled in Chicago.

I sat on the floor in front of a sagging box, blackened on the bottom from mildew and eaten away in spots by a squirrel, and began to unpack it, setting aside a stack of five-year diaries — fastidious chronicles by Ros's mother of her family's daily life in Auburn. Peter absently combed through some business documents of his great-grandfather's, a man named Sam Perry, who — I soon learned — was one of Denver's "empire builders," a financier of the railroad that Dorothy and Ros rode over the Continental Divide. Rob sat on the edge of the bed and talked about childhood visits to their grandmother's rustic summer cabin in the hills of Strawberry Park outside Steamboat Springs. Then my husband handed me a two-page typewritten letter. In the upper-right corner, it said, "Saturday Night. Aug. 6." I looked at the closing: "Dotty and I can hardly believe that this school is really ours to command! . . . Lovingly ROSAMOND."

Ros's entire correspondence was there, each letter typed, folded, and numbered by her mother. The letters had been written to her parents, who, like Dorothy's, had left them for her children and grandchildren. Unwinding the string of a thick legal envelope, I looked inside. It contained dozens of articles and letters from October 1916. They confirmed the most improbable of all the tales my grandmother had told us, about the violent kidnapping of one of their friends. Sensational headlines were spread across the front pages from Denver to Los Angeles: HOW THE MILLIONAIRE'S SON WAS KIDNAPPED AND HELD FOR RANSOM; EXTRA! KIDNAPPER IS SLAIN.

All of these papers and recollections, with

their idiosyncratic details about the "settling up" of northwestern Colorado, provided a backstory to America's leap into the twentieth century. And they filled out the saga about two cosseted women from New York who shunned convention to head out to what was still, in many ways, the Wild West.

■ ■ ■ ■

PART ONE:
BEGINNINGS

■ ■ ■ ■

Dorothy in 1899, age twelve

1
OVERLAND JOURNEY

Hayden, c. 1913

July 27, 1916

A passenger train pulled into the Hayden depot at 10:45 P.M. with a piercing squeal of brakes, a long whistle, and the banging of steel shoes against couplers. The ground shook as the train settled on the tracks, releasing black plumes from the smokestack and foggy white steam from the side pipes. The Denver, Northwestern & Pacific Railway, popularly known as the Moffat Road, had reached Hayden just three years earlier. Until then, Colorado's Western Slope was accessible only by stagecoach, wagon, horseback, and foot. Despite the hulking locomotive, the train didn't look quite up to the twelve-hour journey it had just made over some of the most treacherous passes and peaks of the Rocky Mountains. It consisted of four cars with an observation deck attached at the end. Inside the parlor car, several passengers remained. Hayden was the second-to-last stop on the line.

Dorothy Woodruff and Rosamond Underwood, seasoned travelers in Europe but new to the American West, peered out the window into a disconcerting darkness, unsure whether it was safe to step outside. Then the door of the compartment opened, and a friendly voice called out, "Are you Miss Woodruff and Miss Underwood?" The voice belonged to their employer, Farrington Carpenter. Just a few weeks earlier, he had hired them to teach for the year at a new schoolhouse in the Elkhead Mountains, north of town. His letters, written from his law office in Hayden, were full of odd, colorful descriptions of Elkhead and the children — about thirty students, from poor homesteading families, ranging in age from six to nineteen. Carpenter had assured them it was not a typical one-room schoolhouse. It had electric lights, and the big room was divided by a folding wooden partition, so that each of them could have her own classroom. The basement contained a furnace, a gymnasium, and a domestic science room. Notwithstanding its remote location, he boasted, it was the most modern school in all of Routt County — an area of two thousand square miles.

Ros observed with surprise that "Mr. Carpenter" was a "tall, gangly youth." He wore workaday trousers, an old shawl sweater, and scuffed shoes. She subsequently discovered that he had graduated from Princeton in 1909, the same year she and Dorothy had from Smith. But when they were traveling around Europe and studying French in Paris, he was homesteading in Elkhead. In 1912 he had earned a law degree at Harvard. He retrieved their suitcases from the luggage rack and helped them down the steep steps, explaining that the electricity in Hayden, a recent amenity, had been turned off at ten P.M., as it was every night.

The baggage man heaved their trunks onto the platform, and Carpenter assessed the cargo. Dorothy and Ros had been punctilious in their preparations for the journey, packing suitcases full of books and the two "innovation trunks," which stood up when opened and served as makeshift closets, holding dresses and skirts on one side and bureau drawers on the other. Although they had consulted several knowledgeable people about the proper supplies and clothing, their parents kept urging them to take more provisions. Ros later commented that they were treated as if they were going to the farthest reaches of Africa. Their trunks were almost the size of the boxcar in front of them, which, the women could now make out, was the extent of the depot. Carpenter told them that a wagon would come by the next morning to retrieve the trunks. As he picked up their bulging suitcases and set off, Dorothy suggested sheepishly that he leave them with the trunks. He replied, "Well, no one would get far with them!"

Dorothy and Ros liked him immediately. He staggered down the wooden sidewalk along Poplar Street to the Hayden Inn, followed closely by the ladies. Ros wrote to her parents the next morning, "Why he didn't pull his arms out of their sockets before reaching here, I don't know." There was no reception desk at the Hayden Inn, and no proprietor. Putting down the suitcases inside the cramped entryway, Carpenter turned up a kerosene lamp on the hall table and promised to meet them at breakfast. They found a note by the lamp: "Schoolteachers, go upstairs and see if anyone is in Room 2. If they are, go to Room 3, and if 3 is filled, go to Room 4." When Dorothy cracked open the door to Room 2, she could see that it was occupied, so they crept along the hall to the back of the house and found that the next room — "the bridal suite" — was empty. "We went to bed," Ros said, "glad to be there after that long trip."

They had said goodbye to their parents at New York Central Station in Auburn five days earlier. Auburn, a city of about thirty thousand people in the Finger Lakes district, was one of the wealthiest in the state. Ros's father, George Underwood, was a county judge, and Dorothy's, John Hermon Woodruff, owned Auburn Button Works, which made pearl and shellac buttons, butt plates for rifles, and later, 78-rpm records. The Button Works and the Logan silk mills, jointly owned by Dorothy's father and a maternal uncle, were housed in a factory about a mile north of the Woodruffs' house. They were two of the town's early "manu-factories." Others produced rope, carpets, clothes-wringers, farm machinery, and shoes. Auburn's main arteries, Genesee and South streets, which formed a crooked T, were more like boulevards in the residential neighborhoods, lined with slate sidewalks and stately homes. Majestic old elms arched across and met in the middle. The ties within families and among friends were strong, and the local aristocracy perpetu-ated itself through marriage. Men returned from New York City after making money in banking or railroads; opened law practices and businesses in town; or worked with their brothers and fathers, cousins and uncles. Some never left home at all. Sons and daughters inherited their elders' names and their fortunes. Most women married young and began building their own families. One chronicler observed, "Prick South Street at one end, and it bleeds at the other."

Dorothy, less composed and orderly than Rosamond, had arrived at the station only moments before the train left for Chicago, and as she climbed aboard, she could almost hear her mother saying "I told you so" about the importance of starting in plenty of time. Her last glimpse of her parents was of her father's reassuring smile. He and Ros's mother championed their adventure. Her mother and Ros's father, though, were convinced their daughters would be devoured by wild animals or attacked by Indians. When Ros showed her father one of Carpenter's letters, he turned away and put up his hand, saying, "I don't want to read it."

The girls prevailed, as they invariably did, when their parents saw they were determined to go through with their plans. As Mrs. Underwood put it, "They were fully competent to decide this question." Although intent on their mission, they had bouts of overwhelming nervousness about what they had taken on. During the ride to Chicago, they took notes from the books on teaching that Dorothy had borrowed from a teacher in the Auburn schools. They also reread the letter they had received the previous week from Carpenter:

My dear Miss Woodruff and Miss Underwood,

I was out to the new school house yesterday getting a line on how many pupils there would be, what supplies and repairs we would need etc. . . . I have not heard from you in regard to saddle ponies, but expect you will want them and am looking for some for you. . . .

I expect you are pretty busy getting ready to pull out. If you have a 22 you had better bring it out as there are lots of young sage chicken to be found in that country and August is the open season on them.

With best regards to you both
I am very truly
Farrington Carpenter

They were met at the Chicago station by J. Platt Underwood, an uncle of Ros's, who was, Dorothy observed, "clad in a lovely linen suit." A wealthy timber merchant, he did much of his business in the West, and when they told him that Carpenter had advised them to bring along a rifle, he agreed it was a good idea. The next morning he took them from his house on Lake Park Avenue into the city to buy a .22 and a thousand rounds of shot. It was already 90 degrees downtown and exceedingly humid. Dorothy wrote to her mother that everyone laughed when she tried to pick up the rifle. "I could hardly lift the thing. . . . Imagine what I'll be in Elkhead!" She had better luck at Marshall Field's, where she found a lovely coat: "mixed goods — very smart lines & very warm for $30.00." She and Ros bought heavy breeches at the sport store and got some good leather riding boots that laced up the front.

The oppressive heat wave followed them as they left Chicago, and it got worse across the Great Plains, clinging to their skin along with the dust. Although transportation and safety had improved since the opening of the West, and there were settlements and farms along the railway, the scenery, if anything, was starker than ever. When they were several hundred miles from Denver, there were few signs of life. The riverbeds were cracked open, and there was no long, lush prairie grass or even much sagebrush, just furze and rush and yucca. The few trees along the occasional creeks and "dry rivers" were stunted. The Cheyenne and Arapaho and the awkward, hunchbacked herds of buffalo that had filled the landscape for miles at a stretch were gone. From the train window, Dorothy and Ros caught only an occasional glimpse of jackrabbits.

They had not been aware of the gradual rise in terrain, but they were light-headed as they stepped into the Brown Palace Hotel in Denver. Ros was tall, slender, and strikingly pretty, with a gentle disposition and a poised, steady gaze — "the belle of Auburn," as Dorothy proudly described her. Dorothy's own round, cheerful face was animated by bright blue eyes and a strong nose and chin. People tended to notice her exuberant nature more than her small stature. Under their straw hats, their hair had flattened and was coming unpinned.

Half a dozen well-dressed gentlemen sat in the lobby on tufted silk chairs, reading newspapers or talking; women were relaxing in the ladies' tearoom. A haberdashery and a barbershop flanked the Grand Staircase, and across the room was a massive pillared fireplace made of the same golden onyx as the walls. The main dining room, with gold-lacquered chairs and eight-foot potted palms, was set for dinner. As they approached the reception desk, they saw that the atrium soared above the Florentine arches of the second story. Each of the next six floors was wrapped in an ornate cast-iron balcony, winding up to a stained-glass ceiling. The filtered light it provided, along with the high wall sconces, was pleasantly dim, and it was relatively cool inside.

Ros signed the register for both of them — Miss D. Woodruff and Miss R. Underwood — in neat, girlish handwriting, with none of the sweeping flourishes of the male guests who had preceded them from Kansas City, Philadelphia, Carthage, and Cleveland. On a day when they would have welcomed a strong rain, they were courteously asked whether they preferred the morning or afternoon sun. A bellman showed them to Room 518, with a southeastern exposure and bay windows overlooking the Metropole Hotel and the Broadway Theatre. They were delighted to see that they also had a private bathroom with hot and cold running water. Each of them took a blissful bath, and despite Dorothy's assurances to her mother after her purchases at Field's ("Nothing more for nine months!"), they went straight to Sixteenth Street to shop. They had no trouble finding one of the city's best department stores, Daniels & Fisher. Modeled after the Campanile at the Piazza San Marco, it rose in stately grandeur high above the rest of downtown.

Denver was up-to-date and sophisticated. Its public buildings and best homes were well designed, on a grand, sometimes boastful scale. The beaux arts Capitol — approached by paved sidewalks and a green park — had a glittering gold-leaf dome. There was a financial district on Seventeenth Street known as "the Wall Street of the West"; a YMCA; a Coca-Cola billboard; electric streetcars; and thousands of shade trees. Under the beautification plan of Mayor Robert Speer, the city had imported oaks, maples, Dutch elms, and hackberries, which were irrigated with a twenty-four-mile ditch carrying water from the streams and rivers of the Rockies. The desert had been transformed into an urban oasis.

Dorothy and Ros had heard about the Pike's Peak gold rush of 1859, and they could see how quickly the city had grown up, but beyond that, their knowledge of early Western history was hazy. It was hard to imagine that not even sixty years earlier, Denver City, as it was then called, was a mining camp with more livestock than people. Still part of Kansas Territory, it consisted of a few hundred tents, log cabins, Indian lodges, and shops huddled on the east bank of Cherry Creek by the South Platte River. The cottonwoods along the creek were chopped down for buildings and fuel. Pigs wandered freely in search of garbage. Earthen roofs dripped mud onto the inhabitants when it rained, and they frequently collapsed. The only hotel was a forty-by-two-hundred-foot log cabin. It had no beds and was topped with canvas.

The more visionary newcomers looked past the squalor. One of them was twenty-eight-year-old William Byers, who started the *Rocky Mountain News.* In his first day's edition of the paper, he declared: "We make our debut in the far west, where the snowy mountains look down upon us in the hottest summer day as well as in the winters cold here where a few months ago the wild beasts and wilder Indians held undisturbed possession — where now surges the advancing wave of Anglo Saxon enterprise and civilization, where soon we fondly hope will be erected a great and powerful state." Already Byers was Colorado's most strident advocate, and he became part of the business and political class that made sure his predictions came true. Thousands of prospectors, stirred by exaggerated tales about gold discoveries, imagined the region as "the new El Dorado."

Few valuable minerals were found at Pike's Peak until long after the gold rush had ended. Nevertheless, in the winter and spring of 1859, the first significant placer deposits were found, in the mountains at Clear Creek, thirty-five miles west of Denver; they were soon followed by finds at Central City, Black Hawk, and Russell Gulch. By the end of the year, a hundred thousand prospectors had arrived.

Denver City became an indispensable rest and supply stop for gold diggers on their way to and from the Rockies, as it was for trail drivers and lumbermen. Wagon trains from Missouri and Kansas came to town filled with everything from picks and wheel rims to dry goods, whiskey, coffee, and bacon. Gold dust was the local currency, carried in buckskin pouches and measured on merchants' scales. There was enough of it to start a building boom in everything from gambling halls to drugstores.

With the accumulation of creature comforts in Denver, some speculators were confident that they could domesticate the mountains, too, with dozens of towns and resorts. In the meantime, men returned with stories of suffering and gruesome deaths in the wilderness. In June 1859 a forest fire swept through the dry pines on gusty winds, killing over a dozen people. Horace Greeley, the editor of the *New York Tribune,* had recently stopped in Denver during his famous "Overland Journey," and he made some harsh but titillating assessments of what he had found. "Within this last week," he reported on June 20, "we have tidings of one young gold seeker committing suicide, in a fit of insanity, at the foot of the mountains; two more found in a ravine, long dead and partially devoured by wolves." A month earlier, a man from Illinois, Daniel Blue, had stumbled into Station 25 of the Leavenworth & Pike's Peak Express, skeletal and nearly blind. He said that he and his brothers and the others in their party had lost their way along the Smoky Hill Route, and their packhorse had wandered off. In mid-March, they had used up their remaining ammunition and food, subsisting for a week on grass, boiled roots, and snow. When one of the group died of starvation, the Blue brothers resorted to cannibalism.

One entrepreneur with grandiose ideas about Colorado's future was Henry C. Brown, a tenacious carpenter who opened a workshop by Cherry Creek and eventually owned and ran the *Denver Tribune* and, with a partner, the Bank of Denver. In 1867, when Denver's power brokers were competing with their counterparts in Golden to be the capital of Colorado Territory, Brown settled the issue by donating ten acres of his 160-acre homestead to the city. He stipulated that the capitol be built on the highest point, envisaging the neighborhood as both the city's commercial center and its finest residential district. The Civil War was over, and influential Coloradans, many from northern states, were firm Republicans. Brown gave the new streets resonant pedigrees: Broadway was surrounded by Lincoln, Sherman, Grant, and Logan.

When Brown was ready to build a luxury hotel, he hired Frank Edbrooke, a young architect from Chicago who had designed Denver's spectacular Grand Opera House and one of its earliest office buildings, which was fronted with plate-glass windows. Edbrooke planned the hotel to fit a large triangular plot that Brown had used as his cow pasture. The project took four years and cost $2 million, including the furnishings and fittings. The Brown Palace opened in 1892, sixteen years after Colorado became the thirty-eighth state.

By the time Dorothy and Rosamond arrived, the hotel presided over Denver's business and theater districts. The Union Pacific Railroad delivered passengers to Union Station at the northwest end of Seventeenth Street, near the original site of Denver City; and automobiles — along with trolleys and bicycles — were replacing horses along Broadway. The new "machines" were unreliable and noisy but left behind none of the bacteria, odors, and mess of manure. Colorado, with its high altitude and dry air, was the Baden-Baden of the United States. Hospitals in Denver specialized in the treatment of tuberculosis, and spas had been built in mountain towns known for their mineral waters. Thanks to the boosterism of the *Rocky Mountain News* and other newspapers, the aggressive advertising campaigns of the railroads, and stories of medicinal miracles in Colorado Springs, Manitou, Steamboat Springs, and Hot Sulphur Springs (a town owned by William Byers), tourism had replaced gold as the state's biggest lure.

The two women from the East were surprised to find themselves gazing at the white peaks and blue skies of the Rockies through a heavy haze that was just as bad as the air in Auburn. The pollution was less noticeable in the summer, when coal wasn't needed for heat, but coal fired the electrical generator of the Brown Palace and other businesses, and half a dozen smelters ran year-round, processing mountain ore into gold and silver and emitting their own noxious odors. As in other industrial cities, plumes of gray-black smoke rose throughout downtown; the Brown Palace already had been sandblasted to remove a dark residue that had settled on its facade. The Denver Tramway Company provided service to the "streetcar suburbs." Businessmen who wanted to escape the grit and crowds at the end of the day moved their families south, east, and west of the city, away from the prevailing north winds.

Rosamond and Dorothy had dinner that evening with Palmer Sabin, the son-in-law of Platt Underwood, and his family. The Sabins must have been charmed by their visitors' gumption and social graces. They were worried, though, about how well the two women would manage in Elkhead. The Western Slope lagged decades behind the Front Range of the Rockies. Although the region had fertile valleys and mineral deposits that exceeded those on the eastern side, an 1880 tourists' guide called it "an unknown land." Denver society referred to it as "the wild country." The mountains where they would be living were far from Hayden and the railroad. Elkhead was not a town; it barely qualified as a settlement. It had several dozen scattered residents, no shops or amenities of any kind, and a brutally punishing climate.

Farrington Carpenter had arranged for them to stay with a family of homesteaders. He wrote to them, "I dropped down onto Calf Creek and took dinner with the Harrisons about 2 miles from the school and

Mrs. Harrison said she would take you to board if I would explain in advance that they do not run a regular boarding place, but are just plain ranch folks. They have a new house and can give you a room together for yourselves. . . . They will charge you $20 per month apiece for board and room. You will be expected to take care of your own room and that price does not include washing. . . ." Palmer's mother, Rosamond said, "was very discouraging about our adventure." She told them, "No Denver girls would go up there in that place. It will be terribly hard."

Friends at home believed they were wasting yet another year. Unlikely to find worthy suitors among the cowboys and merchants of Routt County, they were apparently dooming themselves to be old maids. Dorothy and Ros, however, were more bothered by the idea of settling into a staid life of marriage and motherhood without having contributed anything to people who could benefit from the few talents and experiences they had to offer. The notion of a hard life — for a limited time — was exactly what they had in mind.

"We were nothing daunted," Ros recalled, "and spent the night in grandeur at the

Brown Palace Hotel . . . the hottest night I
ever spent in my life."

2
THE GIRLS FROM AUBURN

Dorothy (front) and Rosamond on Owasco Lake

Dorothy and Ros met in Miss Bruin's kindergarten in 1892. The school, started ten years earlier, was one of the first kindergartens in the United States. Miss Bruin was kind to the children, but they shrank from her hugs and kisses because, Dorothy said, "her face bristled with stiff hairs." Dorothy briefly attended a public school on Genesee Street, but when her parents heard about the outside toilets and the unsanitary water pail with a tin cup fastened to it with a chain, they moved her to a private school that Rosamond was attending. Happy to be with Ros again, she didn't mind her solitary mile-and-a-half walk through the village, but her trips home from the primary school on North Street unnerved her. She had to pass through the business district, which was lined with saloons. They had old-style swing doors and smelled strongly of stale beer. Occasionally in the afternoon, she and her friends saw men stumbling out onto the street, and they would run down the block as fast as they could.

Dorothy had six siblings. Anna, the oldest, was followed by Carl, Hermione, Carrie-Belle, Douglas, Dorothy, and Milly. Their mother, Carrie, Dorothy later said, didn't really understand how babies were conceived. Consumed by her many domestic and philanthropic duties, she had little time for the fancies of young children. "I used to beg my mother to tell me stories about what life was like when she was a little girl and how she lived and what Auburn was like," Dorothy said. "But she never seemed able to do it." She revered her mother, and worried about how frequently she displeased her. One spring day, Dorothy was walking by her older cousin's house on South Street, and noticed the garden was full of blooming hyacinths. "I thought they were perfectly beautiful, and how much my mother would like them," she said. "So I walked up and picked every one, took them home, and proudly gave them to Mother. She was absolutely horrified." Carrie insisted that Dorothy go back and apologize to her cousin. In July 1897, when she was ten years old, her parents went off on an extended holiday, and she and her siblings were left with their nursemaid, Mamie. She wrote a winsome note: "My dear Mama . . . I can't imagine that a week from today you will be away out at sea. I do hope that you won't be seasick and that Papa won't have any occasion to put an umbrella over him. . . . I promise to try my best to mind Mamie, so that when you come back you will find me improved. With millions of love, Dorothy."

Carrie, the image of Victorian rectitude in ornate, high-necked dresses, closely watched the household budget, though immigrant labor was cheap. The staff included several maids, a cook, and a gardener. Carrie lived to be ninety-three, one of her daughters-in-law wrote, "in spite of the vicissitudes of a big family." And she never cooked a meal in her life. "Her theory was that if she didn't know how, someone could always be found to do it for her."

Dorothy's father, a commanding figure with a receding hairline and a bushy walrus mustache, was known in Auburn for his quick wit and his generosity. On his birthday every year, all of the guests would find twenty-dollar gold coins in their napkins. Dorothy looked forward to the formal family dinner each night, seeing it as an opportunity to spend uninterrupted time with her parents and her older brothers and sisters. She particularly liked sitting next to her handsome brother Carl, despite his occasional offhand cruelty. One evening she showed him her new pair of white button boots, and when he teased her about her baby fat, she burst into loud sobs and was sent to her room. There was no discussion about who was to blame. Mrs. Woodruff was a strict disciplinarian, and the children were forbidden to interrupt or ask questions at the table. Nevertheless, Dorothy, the product of a pre-psychoanalytic culture, looked back on her childhood in almost idyllic terms. She said of her father, "We just swallowed everything he said and thought it was perfect."

She spent much of her time with her maternal grandmother, Anna Porter Beardsley, a short, erect woman with a strong but embracing personality. Anna had four colonial governors in her lineage, and Dorothy was expected to know their histories. That branch of the Beardsleys lived in a rambling clapboard Greek Revival house, with extensive formal gardens and a level expanse of lawn on which the family gathered to play croquet. The grounds were kept by a gardener who had a square-trimmed beard, a strong Irish brogue, and always kept a clay pipe in his mouth.

On cool days, Dorothy often found her grandmother reading on her bedroom sofa, a wood fire burning in the fireplace. The room contained a bed, a bureau, and a dressing table, painted a pale green, that Dorothy's grandparents had bought soon after they were married. She was told that the furniture had been made by Italian inmates at the Auburn state prison on the other side of town, and she noticed that they had decorated it in delicate brushstrokes with butterflies, trees, and flowers. In the summer, the gardener lined up tomatoes and peaches to ripen on the railing of a porch off the dressing room.

The drawing room, with a white marble

fireplace and tall windows covered by embroidered French white curtains, was used only for formal occasions, such as funerals and the Beardsleys' holiday dinners. "The Beardsley family and its connections by marriage had grown so large," according to one account of early Auburn, "that when the family Christmas dinner was eventually reduced to twenty-five, it seemed to some of the members so small [as] to be hardly worth having."

Dorothy's mother and father were married in the Beardsley mansion in 1872 near a wooden full-length mirror set on a low marble stand. Her father told her that the only thing he remembered about the wedding was looking into the mirror and seeing the shine on his boots — "not very romantic to my young ears." To Dorothy, the dining room was memorable chiefly for the heating register in the floor, where she and her sisters liked to stand and feel the warm air billow their skirts around their legs. Her grandfather had his own use for the heating vent: a servant warmed his pie on it before it was served to him.

Alonzo Beardsley had an aquiline nose, very blue eyes, a bald pink head with a fringe of white hair, and a trailing white beard on which he was apt to spill food. He and his brother Nelson were among the richest men in Auburn. In 1848, along with several colleagues, they had invested in a cornstarch factory nearby. The many uses for cornstarch — from stiffening shirt collars to thickening blancmange — were just being discovered, and in the decades after the Civil War, the Oswego Starch Factory became the most extensive factory of its kind in the world. Each year it burned six thousand tons of coal and used 701,000 pounds of paper and five million board feet of lumber. After dinner, Alonzo retired to his library, which had a floor-to-ceiling mahogany bookcase with glass panes in the door. The only books Dorothy ever took out were James Fenimore Cooper's novels, and she read them all.

She was happiest when she was with Rosamond. The Underwoods' good spirits were contagious, and Ros, who had three brothers but no sisters, cherished her companionship. Ros's mother, Grace, was almost completely deaf — the result of an attack of scarlet fever when she was thirty. No one took much notice of her handicap, despite the ear trumpet she sometimes used. "Mrs. Underwood was a remarkable mother," Dorothy said with unintended poignancy, "because she was so understanding of children and used to play games with us." Mr. Underwood called her "Dotty with the laughing eyes."

Judge Underwood had a keen sense of humor and was a gifted musician who had taught himself to read music and play the piano. At family gatherings, he produced jingles and poems he had written, and Rosamond loved the evenings "when Papa sat alone at the beautiful Steinway piano, sometimes for hours, roaming over the keyboard. He could pass from jazz to grand opera, from hymns to Gilbert and Sullivan's productions, singing the latter with his good voice." Dorothy remembered that one night, after the judge and Ros and her brothers returned from a musical at the Burtis Opera House, he sat down and played the entire score by heart.

As Dorothy grew up, she absorbed the city's spirit of entrepreneurship and noblesse oblige, along with some of the radical thinking about the rights of blacks and women and the working class that had infiltrated an otherwise conservative stronghold. The children of Auburn's gentry learned most of their American history through stories their parents and grandparents told about the city's prominent citizens. William H. Seward had moved to Auburn as a young man and married the daughter of the judge he had worked for before starting his own law practice. Dorothy's great-uncle Nelson Beardsley later became a partner of Seward's at Seward & Beardsley. One of her aunts, Mary Woodruff, was a good friend of Seward's daughter Fanny.

Seward, the foremost of the Auburn radicals, was short and clean-shaven, with red hair, a raspy voice, and a sharp, swooping nose that prompted Henry Adams to refer to him as "a wise macaw." In 1846, after serving two terms as governor, Seward represented a twenty-three-year-old black man named William Freeman who was charged with stabbing to death a white family of four in nearby Fleming. The victims were a pregnant woman, her husband, her son, and her mother. People in Auburn were stunned by the crime and warned that whoever defended Freeman could expect retribution. As Freeman was escorted to jail, he was almost lynched by a mob.

Seward's wife, Frances, was passionately interested in abolition, women's rights, and her husband's work, and she helped him with his research. Freeman's family had a history of mental illness, but the Sewards believed that he became deranged after repeated beatings in the Auburn prison, where he was held for five years for horse stealing, a crime he almost certainly did not commit.

During the trial, Seward made an early use of the insanity defense. His library on South Street, which today is filled with the pleasant smell of moldering leather bindings, contains a dense volume published in 1845 called *Principles of Forensic Medicine.* One of the passages that Frances marked in the margins with two heavy lines in black ink was "*Non compos mentis* is one of four sorts." In Seward's summation to the jury, he argued: "I am the lawyer for society, for mankind, shocked beyond the power of expression, at the scene I have witnessed here of trying a maniac as a malefactor."

Although he lost the case, he appealed to the New York Supreme Court, which reversed the conviction. Freeman died in prison before a second trial could take place. Seward was out of town, and Frances wrote to him with the news: "Poor Bill is gone at last — he died alone in his cell was found dead this morning. . . . I am glad the suffering of the poor benighted creature is terminated. . . . The good people of Auburn can now rest quietly in their beds 'the murderer' has no longer the power to disturb them."

Seward had earned a national reputation as a man of unimpeachable integrity. Three years later, he began the first of two terms in the U.S. Senate, and after contending unsuccessfully against Lincoln in the 1860 presidential contest, he became the secretary of state. Lincoln liked to call him "Governor," but when Seward returned from Washington, his once disapproving neighbors referred to him respectfully as "the Secretary."

The Sewards provided financial backing for the abolitionist newspaper *North Star,* published out of Rochester by their friend Frederick Douglass. In the 1850s — along with half a dozen or so other Auburn families — they harbored fugitive slaves in their basement. Through their work with the Underground Railroad, they became close to Harriet Tubman, and after the Civil War, they convinced her to settle in Auburn, selling her a wooden house and seven acres a few miles down South Street for her and her relatives. She also looked out for other African-Americans in town, opening the first home in the country for indigent and elderly blacks. When Dorothy and Ros were small, the elderly Tubman rode a bicycle up and down South Street, stopping to ask for food donations. If she had specific needs, she sat on the back porch and waited for the lady of the house, with whom she would chat and ask for bedding or clothing for her residents. One of Ros's nieces said, "Mother had coffee with Harriet and would always leave a ham or turkey for her for the holiday."

The Woodruff fortune rose and fell according to the demand for buttons, so Dorothy's family did not have all of the luxuries the wealthiest families had, such as a summer cottage on Owasco Lake. But Ros's parents did, and Dorothy spent most summers with them. One of the Finger Lakes, Owasco was a few miles south of Auburn. About eleven miles long and three-quarters of a mile wide, it was surrounded by lush and hilly farmland that dropped sharply to a wooded shore. In the summer months, the women and children of Auburn society took advantage of the fresh air and clean water, and the men commuted to Auburn by steamboat or train. People came all the way from New York City to escape the "vapors" and epidemics. The lake also was a popular spot for entertaining U.S. presidents and other dignitaries. In the mid-1800s, there were legendary parties at Willowbrook, the family compound of Enos Throop, New York's tenth governor. Presidents Johnson and Grant and General Custer were among the guests, stopping for a banquet in their honor during Johnson's "Swing Around the Circle" tour in 1866, an unsuccessful effort to boost support for his Reconstruction policies.

Ros's father taught the children to swim, row, and sail. When the girls swam, they wore the heavy bathing costumes of the day: short-sleeved wool dresses to their knees, over drawers and black stockings, and bathing slippers — all topped with oversize caps to protect their hair. The picturesque "Lady of the Lake" steamboat made two round trips a day, delivering groceries, mail, and guests to the cottages. Residents hoisted flags on their docks when they wanted the boat to stop, and, Dorothy said, "No ocean voyage was more thrilling than those trips on our little twelve-mile-long lake."

One summer Dorothy's extended family rented Willow Point, a spacious two-story shingle house owned by a particularly esteemed Auburn couple, David Osborne and his wife, Eliza. The tracks of the Lehigh Valley Railroad ran behind the houses on the lake, and Dorothy remembered that when the freight trains went by, transporting anthracite coal from Pennsylvania to Ontario, they rattled the house.

David Osborne, a friend of the Woodruffs, Underwoods, and Beardsleys, was one of the city's most influential entrepreneurs. His business, D. M. Osborne & Company, sold harvesters, mowers, and other farm equipment. Its phalanxes of factory buildings along Genesee Street had thirty-five hundred employees, and by the turn of the century, it had become the third largest enterprise of its kind in the country.

Eliza Osborne was one of the most prominent suffragists in Cayuga County. Her mother was Martha C. Wright, whom an Auburn neighbor referred to as "a very dangerous woman." Martha Wright organized the 1848 Seneca Falls Convention for women's rights, along with Eliza's aunt Lucretia Mott and Elizabeth Cady Stanton. Eliza was a tall, regal woman whose glorious black eyes, according to Stanton, were brimming with "power and pathos." Ros's mother considered her a close friend, even though Eliza was a generation older. Eliza's father, David Wright, worked with Seward on the defense of William Freeman, and the Wrights, too, hid runaway slaves. Beginning in the 1860s, Eliza Osborne hosted her own meetings with Stanton, Susan B. Anthony, and other feminist leaders at her home on South Street.

When Dorothy was seven years old, Eliza bought her grandfather Woodruff's former property next to the Seward House. For two decades Eliza was the president and principal financial patron of the local chapter of the Woman's Educational and Industrial Union, a group devoted to the moral and social welfare of local working girls. She greatly expanded the house, turning it into the Osborne Memorial Building, an august four-story structure of red brick, for the growing activities of the Woman's Union. It contained a dressmaking classroom, a cooking school, a gymnasium, and a day nursery. Before long, a "swimming tank" was added in a new wing. Many of Auburn's socially prominent women donated money and time to Eliza's undertaking. Eventually, Dorothy and Ros were among them.

Eliza doted on her son Thomas Mott Osborne, who inherited his elders' commitment to political reform and social justice. In middle age, he befriended and advised young Franklin D. Roosevelt. In 1911, when FDR was a twenty-nine-year-old state senator, they worked together to fight the corruption of Tammany Hall. They were also active supporters of Woodrow Wilson's 1912 presidential campaign, lobbying behind the scenes at the Democratic convention in Baltimore; Wilson secured the nomination on the forty-sixth ballot. Osborne was gratified when the new administration appointed Roosevelt assistant secretary of the navy, but he abandoned politics in disgust after many federal appointments went to Tammany Hall and its sympathizers. Instead, Osborne convinced the governor of New York to appoint him chairman of a long overdue state commission on prison reform.

The young ladies of Auburn were mostly protected from the uglier outgrowths of the industrial age, but the state prison, a vast complex on State Street across from the train station, was unavoidable. Auburn's rapid growth from a quiet village on the edge of the American frontier into a major industrial center would not have been possible without it. Two octagonal stone towers framed the main gate, and the high, long walls enclosed a grim collection of cell blocks, workshops, and the administration building, heavily hung with untended ivy.

The prison opened in the early 1800s, and four years later, inmates began providing cheap contract labor — an attraction for fledgling industries. Convicts made steam engines, sleighs, shoes, nails, furniture, and other products. Factories quickly sprang up nearby, along the Owasco Outlet, an excellent source of hydraulic power. Auburn's officials promised an innovative approach to rehabilitation, and their methods, known as "the Auburn system," were admired throughout the country and Europe. So was the prison's intimidating architecture, which became the model for most U.S. penitentiaries.

The Auburn system was designed to instill good behavior through confinement in individual cells, strict discipline, and work at various trades. Silence was maintained at all times. The inmates marched in striped uniforms to workshops in the Auburn-invented "lockstep." Anyone who broke the rule of silence was flogged with the "cat" — a cat-o'-nine tails, with lashes eighteen inches long, made out of waxed shoe thread, which were said to "cut the flesh like 'whips of steel.' " Eventually, the cat was replaced with a three-foot wooden paddle covered with leather. Others were subjected to the "shower bath": stripped, bound, and placed inside a barrel. A wooden collar was fastened around their necks to immobilize their heads as a spigot dispensed ice-cold water. The shower bath was discontinued in

1858 after a prisoner drowned during treatment.

Thomas Mott Osborne often hosted elaborately costumed theatricals at his home, and he had a gift for impersonation. In 1913, a few months after taking the job as prison reform commissioner, he posed for a week as Tom Brown, Inmate #33,333X. When he got out, he and a former prisoner founded the Mutual Welfare League, devising a form of limited self-government in the prison and helping to prepare inmates for life outside. Osborne's work put an end to the rule of silence and secured prisoners the right to go out into the yard for an hour each evening. He wrote a book about the experience, *Within Prison Walls,* and his exploit as an inmate and his reforms were recounted in papers around the world.

Dorothy never fully reconciled the two Auburns. She told her grandchildren about a horrifying early memory: the execution of William McKinley's assassin, Leon Czolgosz, who in 1901 was put to death in the prison, in the world's first electric chair. She was fourteen years old at the time, and some eighty years later, she said she had been upset to hear that there would be no funeral for him; he was to be buried in Fort Hill Cemetery in a far corner in an unmarked grave.

Fort Hill Cemetery, set on eighty-three verdant acres, played a vivid role in her imagination. Fort Street was only one block long, and the Woodruffs lived by the cemetery's entrance. In the sixteenth century, Fort Hill — the highest spot in the vicinity — was a fortified area in a Cayuga Indian village. Dorothy's grandmother Anna had her own story of back-door visitors when she was a child in Auburn: hungry Indians who occasionally appeared outside the kitchen asking for food. The road was steep and winding as it entered the cemetery, and during Auburn's heavy snows, Dorothy and her siblings went sledding there. On weekends in warmer weather, Dorothy and Milly explored the cemetery. Mamie packed their lunches in shoe boxes, which they supplemented in the fall with ripe beechnuts that dropped from the trees. Their sister Hope had died of whooping cough in 1884 when she was six weeks old, and the girls were sentimentally drawn to the graves of children. As soon as they could read, they wandered among the tiny tombstones, making out the dates and the weathered inscriptions.

Dorothy's favorite stop, on a mounded crest of the highest hill, was a fifty-six-foot obelisk, a monument to a Cayuga Indian chieftain known as Logan who was widely admired in the East. Chief Logan was born Tahgahjute, ostensibly on Fort Hill, which the Cayugas called Osco; when he was a young man, his name was changed to Logan, apparently as an homage to Governor William Penn's secretary, James Logan. Judge William Brown of Pennsylvania, reflecting the romantic Victorian view, called Logan "the best specimen of humanity I have ever met with, either white or red." In 1774 Logan's family had been murdered by colonists in Virginia. He organized a retaliatory attack that turned into a series of bloody battles between the settlers and area Indian tribes. Logan refused to attend the peace conference, although he sent an eloquent statement for the occasion, which was described in a history of Auburn as "that masterpiece of oratory which ranks along with the memorable speech of President Lincoln at Gettysburg." Dorothy never forgot the haunting inscription on the Logan memorial, taken from the address: "Who is there to mourn for Logan?"

During Auburn's military funerals for its fallen soldiers, she and Milly sat on the curb in front of their house and watched the aged veterans of the Civil War marching solemnly by in faded uniforms. Dorothy remembered that Brigadier General William H. Seward, Jr., led "a fife and drum corps which used to wail famous funeral marches which I can hear to this day."

Dorothy and Ros were separated for the first time in their third year of high school, when Ros went to Germany with her family. The Underwoods asked Dorothy to join them, and she desperately wanted to go, but she thought that if she didn't apply herself to her schoolwork, she might not get into Smith College, which she and Ros had long planned to attend together. Dorothy's oldest sister, Anna, a brilliant, serious girl with a long, heavy braid down her back, had gone to Smith in 1893 — a major event in the family. Few women went to college, and Dorothy was prepared to sacrifice for that experience. Nevertheless, she came to rue her decision to stay home.

While Ros was becoming worldly — learning German, traveling to Greece, and journeying up the Nile in a dahabeah — Dorothy was attending Rye Seminary, a girls' boarding school on the Boston Post Road in Rye, New York. The school gave its students a sober Christian education, with an emphasis on college preparatory work. Although it eventually morphed into the well-appointed Rye Country Day School, it was a spartan place early in the twentieth century. At mealtime, the girls clattered down the iron stairs into the basement, where the French teacher presided over one table and the German teacher the other, and no English was spoken. As a result, conversations were halting and garbled. Dorothy shared a large bedroom with two other girls. Each had an iron bed and a washstand, and there was also a piano in the room. Girls were excused from class for their weekly baths. A schedule was posted on the bathroom door at the end of the hall.

In her letters home, Dorothy wrote about extracurricular activities off school grounds. In 1903, when she was sixteen, she described a day in New York, where she and her classmates went to Wagner's *Die Walküre*. "Oh, Grandma," she wrote, "I have just come home, and the opera was the most wonderful thing I have ever seen. I was afraid that it would be deep and perhaps it was, but I never enjoyed anything so much in all my life." The next fall, she told about a trip with her friends to Lakehurst, New Jersey. The girls stayed at a beautiful inn where, she wrote, "the spirit is so lovely that it doesn't seem a bit like a hotel." They played tennis, danced, and took walks in the woods.

At Thanksgiving, Dorothy and three other girls were invited to a friend's house near Port Chester, and she wrote to her mother on November 27 about their trip into Manhattan, where they shopped at Altman's, had lunch, and went to the Hudson Theater to see *Sunday*. "Ethel Barrymore is simply perfect," she announced, "and I am crazy about her."

Although Dorothy said she didn't learn much at Rye, she was strongly influenced by one teacher who sometimes invited her to her room, where she served little cakes and pastries and gave her books of poetry by Shelley and Keats. "I just loved her," Dorothy said, "and this is a perfect example of what a good teacher can do to stimulate a growing young person's mind and imagination."

3
"A Funny, Straggly Place"

Ferry Carpenter in his law office

On the morning after their arrival in Hayden, Dorothy and Ros woke up early. They would be leaving in several hours for Elkhead, in the mountain range that abutted the Yampa Valley, and as Dorothy recalled, "We could hardly wait to see what was in store for us." When they walked into the dining room, half a dozen cowboys were seated at a large round table. "Of course nobody got up or anything, they simply stared at us." As they sat down, the man next to her said, "Good morning, ma'am." He was wearing a boiled white shirt with no collar, and a diamond stud in the neckband. The table was covered with hot cereals and biscuits and jams and coffee, and she and Ros ordered eggs, "once over, in the most approved manner." Then "started a great procession of right and left," as the men passed the food around, so persistently that it was hard to eat. The women tried to make conversation, "but all we got out from anybody was 'Yes, ma'am' and 'No, ma'am' or 'I wouldn't know, ma'am,' " and when they handed a dish to a neighbor, he would say, " 'I wouldn't wish to care for any, thank you, ma'am.' "

Their breakfast companions bore no resemblance to the refined young men they were accustomed to. Nor did Farrington Carpenter, who soon came in, introduced them to the cowboys, and said he had two ponies for them, as well as a conveyance to take them to the Harrison ranch. "We are tremendously impressed by Mr. C., who is a big man," Dorothy wrote that morning.

"He has a gentle, kindly manner, with keen eyes, a fine sense of humor and a regular live wire along every line." He took them to his office to talk everything over, and Dorothy — not wanting to confirm her mother's preconceptions about the uncouth West — avoided any mention of the office's history as a one-lane bowling alley, the electrical cord dangling from the ceiling to Carpenter's desk lamp, or the homely floral curtains.

Instead, she wrote: "His library was perfectly amazing, it showed such broad up-to-date interests, and we are certainly going to have to work night and day to keep up our end." His books included a complete set of Shakespeare, *The Life of David Crockett, An Autobiography,* a collection of Ralph Waldo Emerson's essays and lectures, *The Greek View of Life,* a biography of Walt Whitman, a six-volume edition of the poetry of Robert Burns, several biographies of Abraham Lincoln, *The Colorado Justice Manual,* and a book called *Swine,* a breeding and feeding guide. They spent two hours discussing their work at the school, and Ros wrote that morning with undisguised relief: "He is anxious to have us run the whole thing as we want to run it — and says we don't have to teach Domestic Science if we don't want to — or Sunday School either." She and Dorothy, having grown up in households staffed by maids and cooks, were more nervous about teaching domestic science, a turn-of-the-century precursor to home economics, than any other subject. "We didn't know anything about domestic science," Ros later admitted.

As for Hayden, Dorothy wrote, it was "a funny, straggly place," and its residents "snappy and entertaining," their good manners "as surprising as the kind of English they speak." Neither of them mentioned the cowboys in the dining room. Ros wrote, "The air is like tonic — and we are cool at last after dreadful heat in Denver. The country here is flat — with blue mountains in the country towards we go." Dorothy's pony was a sorrel called Nugget, on loan from Carpenter. She said he "is so little that I can hop off and on with the greatest ease." Ros's horse came from Steamboat Springs, and she was to name him herself.

At Earnest Wagner's saddle shop, they rented saddles and bought bits, bridles, ropes, spurs, and ponchos, then shook hands with all of the townspeople in the street. "We were introduced to each one, who gave us a terrible grip with their horny paws," Dorothy wrote innocently. As they were about to embark on their long, dusty ride to Elkhead, Ros scribbled: "Mr. C. has just telephoned that he is coming to lunch with us, and start us on our way — so no more now. Rosamond."

Straggly Hayden, like so many western towns, had come into being quickly and violently. Among its first settlers was the extended family of Porter M. Smart, the superintendent of the Western Colorado Improvement Company. In December 1874, the *Rocky Mountain News* referred to Smart as "one of that peculiar and persevering class of pioneers who are always in the van of civilization." He had built his house in "the remotest settlement of Western Colorado." That winter, his son Albert took in a few families who had been unable to provide for themselves, and one man began to steal flour, bacon, and groceries. The "culprit was arrested, tried, convicted, tied up to a tree and 'larruped' with long switches, and then given forty-eight hours to leave the country. He left." The *News* declared, "The company of which Mr. Smart is the representative is doing a world of good in thus extending family altars into the wilderness."

The Smarts and their few neighbors were

sometimes visited by Ute Indians, members of a nomadic tribe whose name for the Rockies was "the shining mountains." They had inhabited the land for over five hundred years. In return for dinner and a few sacks of potatoes, the Utes offered game and buckskins. But relations with the Utes became difficult over the next several years, as miners and merchants began to settle in the region.

Like the early gold prospectors in Denver, people rushed out after learning of the region's natural resources. This time the riches were publicized almost single-handedly by one man: Ferdinand Vandeveer Hayden, the world-famous geologist who in 1871 had led an expedition to survey all of Yellowstone country, and helped convince Congress to establish it as the first national park. Hayden spent the summers of 1873–75 conducting a similarly exhaustive study of the Colorado Rockies. One of his teams of surveyors, photographers, and scientists, working for the Department of the Interior, camped by the Bear River, near where the Smarts lived; the surveyors' mail was addressed simply to "Hayden Camp."

A thin, obsessive scholar with dark pouches under his eyes and an irascible disposition, Hayden had a genius for transforming highly technical geographical and geological data into popular science. He also was an outspoken advocate of development, writing to the secretary of the Interior Department about how rapidly the region would grow with the coming of the railroads, thus rendering it "very desirable that its resources be made known to the world at as early a date as possible." He gave lectures in Washington and New York in the mid-1870s about his discoveries of fantastic geysers and bubbling gray mud pots in Yellowstone, and hidden valleys with thriving communities in the Rockies. The talks included slides by a member of his team, the renowned photographer William H. Jackson, projected on a stereopticon. Hayden's *Atlas of Colorado,* published in 1877, was glowingly written about in both the United States and Europe. William Blackmore, a British investor in American ventures, claimed that English schoolboys couldn't name the presidents, but "all knew intimately the stories of Dr. Hayden's expeditions in to the wild Indian country of the far West."

The atlas gorgeously laid out every feature of the state in a succession of oversize maps showing its topography, drainage, geology — and its economic resources, including

"Gold and Silver Districts" and "Coal Lands." The region west of the Divide was densely speckled with prospective mining sites. The atlas also revealed how much of that land the Utes controlled, according to a treaty signed in 1873: twelve million acres on the Western Slope — over half of the Colorado Rockies. Two pages of the atlas, showing northwestern Colorado, were marked with large capital letters crossing the book's gutter and filling almost the entire map: RESERVATION OF THE UTE INDIANS.

By the late 1870s, Colorado's second mining boom was well under way, and Leadville and other camps were built on Ute territory. The Utes rebelled, setting fires to settlers' homes and to timber and prairie grass. This fueled a propaganda campaign in the pages of the *Denver Tribune,* with the slogan "The Utes Must Go!" Governor Frederick W. Pitkin emphatically shared that view, and did his part to encourage the growing public uproar.

The most serious trouble between the settlers and the Utes was precipitated by Nathan Meeker, head of the White River Agency, forty-five miles southwest of Hayden. Meeker was attempting to build a model agricultural community, teaching the

Indians to become good farmers and Christians; educating their children; and disabusing them of numerous uncivilized practices. The Ute men, though, believed that farming was women's work and that horses were not meant to pull a plow but to be ridden and raced. They despised Meeker, with his arrogant paternalism and his threatening claim that the U.S. government owned their land.

The Utes in Yampa Valley appealed for help to Major James B. Thompson, who ran a trading post by the Bear River and had won their trust. In response, Thompson, Smart, and the other settlers sent a petition to the Interior Department, asking for an investigation of Meeker and for protection for their families. Troops were sent, but to Hot Sulphur Springs, the closest town, about a hundred miles southeast. Porter Smart's daughter-in-law Lou, the mother of four children and pregnant with her fifth, was visited repeatedly by Utes in June 1879 when her husband, Albert, was away. She wrote in a letter afterward that they demanded food and matches, and that one of them wanted to trade back a gun that Albert had given him in exchange for a pony: " 'The gun no good. Would not kill buckskin, wanted trade back, give five dollars

74

take pony go away no trouble squaw.' "

That summer, she said, she had "another dreadful miscarriage, worse even than the last." For ten days she couldn't sit up in bed. The Utes returned, camping near the house. When they heard that a company of Negro soldiers — Company D of the Ninth Cavalry — was not far away, waiting for orders, "They said they didn't care how many white men came but they wouldn't stand Negroes (that was too great an insult)." They set fire to two houses before riding off.

In August, after an altercation with the Utes' medicine man at the White River Agency, Meeker, claiming serious injuries, requested that Governor Pitkin send troops for his protection. Pitkin, a former mining investor and one of the more unscrupulous proponents of Manifest Destiny, had long argued that, treaty or not, the situation with the Utes was untenable. A few weeks later, three cavalry companies crossed onto Ute land at Milk Creek, the northern border of the reservation; about a dozen soldiers were killed and many more injured. The ambush came to an end when Company D arrived to rescue the men, but the White River Utes turned on Meeker, shooting him in the head, burning his farm to the ground, and abducting his wife and daughter.

Major Thompson, anticipating disaster, had already left. The Smarts and other families hurriedly packed their belongings and moved out. They stopped at Steamboat Springs, which consisted of little more than the homestead of James Crawford, the town's founder. They barricaded themselves in at the Crawfords' cabin for a few days, continuing on to Hot Sulphur Springs when it seemed safe. They arrived ten days after leaving home. Lou Smart and her husband learned that their house had been robbed of everything edible; chicken bones and feathers were scattered about inside. She said she feared that the Ute war had only just begun, yet she went on, "The only thing that worries me is the children not having any schooling, especially Charlie. There is no school here and they say there is to be none this winter." Lou Smart died a few months later of complications from her miscarriage.

The Meeker Massacre, as newspapers across the country labeled it, gave Governor Pitkin an opportunity to make a special announcement to the press about the Ute threat: "My idea is that, unless removed by the government, they must necessarily be exterminated." He pointed out "The advan-

76

tages that would accrue from the throwing open of twelve million acres of land to miners and settlers. . . ." In August 1881 the U.S. Army force-marched virtually all of the Colorado Utes 350 miles to a reservation on a desolate stretch of land near Roosevelt, Utah.

As the Utes were being dispensed with, the settlement by the Bear River grew. A log school and a store were built on the homestead of Sam and Mary Reid, who had moved to the valley in 1880. Mary became postmistress the following year. The mail came by buckboard from Rawlins, Wyoming, three times a week, and the mailman crossed the river in a canoe. Sam Reid's brother-in-law, William Walker, moved from North Carolina; several years later, he was joined by his wife and children. They homesteaded on a parcel of land just north of town previously held by Albert Smart. A man named Ezekiel Shelton, trained as an engineer in Ohio, was sent to Yampa Valley by some Denver businessmen in 1881 to investigate stories of coal beds in the Elkhead Mountains. His reports were positive, and so was his response to the valley. Shelton helped establish the Hayden Congregational Church, to which one of the settlement's first three women, Mrs. Emma Peck, donated her organ. Shelton and Emma Peck even started a tiny literary society. Other pioneers followed, and the town of Hayden was incorporated in March 1906, when Farrington Carpenter and Ros and Dorothy were in their first year of college.

4
"REFINED, INTELLIGENT GENTLEWOMEN"

Dorothy and Rosamond at Smith

One Sunday afternoon that month, Dorothy got a letter from her father, reminding her to dedicate herself to her studies at Smith. "We follow your life at College as reflected in your letters with deep interest & while you evidently enjoy the days as they

79

pass I doubt not you are doing your work — I want you to master your French so that you can make it practical, learn to converse fluently. . . ."

Smith students were caught between the college's aspirations for them and the social mores of the day — some of which the school administration shared. Not all of the women made it through four years. Seventy-five of Dorothy and Ros's classmates, about a fifth of the class of 402, withdrew before commencement. One graduate wrote a "Senior Class history of 1909" for the yearbook, in which she coyly presented their dilemma as they entered the world: "We have not yet decided whether to 'come out' in society or 'go in' for settlement work." Jane Addams had started Hull House, the country's first settlement house, in Chicago in 1889. The underprivileged, regardless of race or ethnicity, took advantage of its social services, including school for their children and night classes for themselves. Addams had longed to go to Smith, to prepare for a career in medicine, but her father wouldn't allow it; he believed that her duty was to serve her family. In the years after his death, she became known across the country for her advocacy for civil rights, unions, female suffrage, and an end to child labor. To many college women, she was a model of enlightened thought and industry.

Yet, the Smith graduate continued in the yearbook, "Unlike our neighbor Holyoke 'over the way,' we have not troubled our busy heads over the right and wrong of woman suffrage, but are discussing whether psyches make long noses look longer and just who *are* the best-looking girls in the class. Some of us are hoping for an M.A., others, to quote a scintillating Junior, are hoping for a M.A.N. A few of us look, may look, forward to getting Ph.D.'s after our names, a few more of us, however, are looking forward to getting M-r-s. in front of them."

Smith College, started by Sophia Smith, a maiden lady who lived in Hatfield, near Northampton, was young: chartered in 1871, it opened in 1875. The only other full-fledged women's colleges in the country at that time were Elmira, Mary Sharp, and Vassar. Mount Holyoke and Wellesley were still known as female seminaries, where students attended Bible-study groups, church services, chapel talks, and prayer meetings. Twice a day they performed private devotions. Wellesley Female Seminary changed its name to Wellesley College in 1875, and Mount Holyoke, eighteen years later. The pastor of Sophia Smith's church had repeatedly urged her to pursue the idea of a college for women, and three months before her death, she made a codicil to her will in which she declared her belief that a higher Christian education for women would be the best way to redress their wrongs and to increase their wages and their "influence in reforming the evils of society . . . as teachers, as writers, as mothers, as members of society."

This belief — that women and men should be educated in separate colleges — was not widely shared among public intellectuals along the Eastern Seaboard. Henry Ward Beecher, for one, thought that the solution to higher education for women was to admit them to men's colleges, a practice already being followed in the Midwest and the West. (Oberlin became the first coeducational college in the country in 1837, when it enrolled four women. Two years earlier, it had admitted its first African-American students.) At Amherst's semicentennial celebration in July 1871, Beecher gave a speech in which he pressed his alma mater to admit women. So did the former governor of Massachusetts. Lengthy deliberations followed at Amherst and at Yale, Harvard, Williams, and Dartmouth, but the notion was not pursued at any of these colleges for another century. When Radcliffe College opened in 1879, it was known as "the Harvard Annex."

The president and trustees of Smith were clear about their mission. In June 1877, while Lou Smart was negotiating trades with the Utes in Yampa Valley, President L. Clark Seelye wrote in an annual circular in Northampton, "It is to be a woman's college, aiming not only to give the broadest and highest intellectual culture, but also to preserve and perfect every characteristic of a complete womanhood." He often said that one of Smith's missions was to teach its students to become "refined, intelligent gentlewomen."

The college intended to provide a curriculum just as rigorous as that of the best men's schools, but Seelye conceded that many of the students were not entirely ready for the academic demands. He and his successor expected Smith to stimulate students' intellectual curiosity and help them develop an appreciation of the scientific method. However, since most of them had "neither the call nor the competence to devote their lives to research," they were encouraged to work on "the development of the character and capacities of the personality."

The exceptions were notable. After graduation, Jane Kelly, Class of 1888, went to Northwestern University Women's Medical School and then to Johns Hopkins for a year of postgraduate work in medicine — there, she was required to sit in the balcony behind a curtain during lectures. She established both a medical practice and a family in Boston. After a week at Wood's Hole in the summer of 1902, she wrote to her classmates, "There was a large number of Smith girls working in the Laboratories, which speaks well for the scientific spirit fostered in our Alma Mater."

Dorothy did not have that calling. She had graduated from Rye Seminary with strong grades and managed to pass Smith's entrance examinations, which included translating English sentences into Greek, Latin, French, and German, and — in the English section — writing on the themes of *Julius Caesar, The Vicar of Wakefield,* and *Silas Marner,* and on the form and structure of *Macbeth, Lycidas, L'Allegro,* and other texts. She was not strongly motivated, though, and claimed that Rye had not taught her how to study. "The fact that I'd gone to Smith College to learn, I don't think made much impression on me," she said. The first semester, she got the equivalent of Ds in her two English classes, C- in French, B- in

German, C- in Latin, and C+ in mathematics. She was put on probation. Ros did better, with a C, two B-'s, a B, and two A's. Dorothy's record improved somewhat as the semesters wore on, but she never excelled and was not overly concerned about her grades.

She had warm recollections of one teacher at Smith, just as she'd had at Rye. In her junior and senior years, she took European history with Charles Hazen, whom she described as the first teacher she'd ever had who "could make you live the way those characters lived so long ago and the events in history seem so real." Dorothy's fascination with the past, sparked in Auburn and revived by Hazen, stayed with her throughout her life.

Admitting that her academic performance over her four years was undistinguished, she described herself as "romping" through Smith: "I loved every minute . . . I was invited to join all of the fun and social clubs that there were." She and Ros both belonged to the Phi Kappa Psi Society, the Current Events Club, and the Novel Club (its goals were to write a good novel and to have a good time, no one seemed to bother with the novel). She was a "tumble bug" at the Junior Frolic event at "the Hippodrome" and helped design costumes for the senior production of *A Midsummer Night's Dream.* Ros was a member of the Smith College Council. Their friendship was no less close in those years; it simply expanded to include others. "Life was very relaxed and easy," Dorothy noted. "Although of course we studied, we nevertheless had plenty of time to be with each other." They kept in touch with their Smith friends for sixty years.

When it came time to choose an "invitation house," Ros joined the White Lodge, and Dorothy agonized between that and Delta Sigma, which was, one of its founding members emphasized, not a secret society or a sorority — a distinction, perhaps, without a difference. The invitation houses cost more than campus housing, but along with an exclusive circle of friends, they promised single rooms, a housekeeper, a cook, a waitress, and some freedom not allowed on campus. Dorothy wryly described the choice between the two houses as "really one of the great problems of my young life — what I should do about this."

She joined Delta Sigma as a sophomore, and she idolized the juniors and seniors — "I thought they were the most beautiful and brilliant creatures on earth." The members had recently moved into a yellow clapboard house off Main Street, with a welcoming veranda and a spacious side porch that had two long wooden swings, cushioned in chintz and suspended from the ceiling by chains. The living room had a large fireplace, which was lit on chilly days after lunch. Sixteen students ate their meals at a long table in the dining room, presided over by the house matron. When they invited President Seelye or professors to dinner, dessert was the Faculty Cake, filled with macaroons, sherry, and whipped cream. The girls managed the household budget and were expected to observe the college's "ten o'clock rule" at bedtime. The college held dances, but they were women-only. Students were allowed to invite gentlemen to the Junior Promenade, the Rally on Washington's Birthday, and the Glee Club Concert.

Dorothy and Ros played gentle games of tennis in white skirts sweeping their ankles, and planned off-campus activities, including picnics. They took the trolley out Main Street to the end of the line in Greenfield, and walked through the woods to a brook, where they gathered twigs and built a fire. They roasted sausages called "bacon bats" on forked sticks, which they ate on buttered rolls, and they made coffee in a tin pail. For longer trips, they rented an old horse and wagon and rode out into the country, occasionally stopping for a night or two at one of the farmhouses.

Several weeks before graduation, Dorothy wrote to her grandmother. She and some friends had visited Deerfield's Memorial Hall, a museum that contained relics from the French and Indian Raid of 1704. Referring to the sacking of the town and the letters written from Canada by captured French officers to their families, she observed: "The village is so little and sleepy, and still so much in the country, that it required very little imagination to take us back to those times." The girls had supper by "that same brook, which has seen so many awful things," she wrote, "but I never saw more wonderful country. The mountains are so very green, dotted here and there with fruit trees and the air heavy with the odor of lilacs."

There is no indication that either Dorothy or Ros had in mind anything more taxing for their futures than the kind of charity work pursued by their friends and mothers in Auburn. Nor were they intent on finding husbands, not having met any young men whose company they liked nearly as much as they liked each other's. Dorothy told her grandmother how much she appreciated the